ENDANGERED
OCEAN ANIMALS

Dave Taylor

Crabtree Publishing Company

Endangered Animals Series

Text and photographs by Dave Taylor

To Don, who also thought I could do it

Editor-in-chief
Bobbie Kalman

Editors
Janine Schaub
David Schimpky

Cover mechanicals
Rose Campbell

Design and computer layout
Antoinette "Cookie" DeBiasi

Separations and film
EC Graphics Ltd.

Printer
Worzalla Publishing

Published by
Crabtree Publishing Company

350 Fifth Avenue	360 York Road, RR4	73 Lime Walk
Suite 3308	Niagara-on-the-Lake	Headington
New York	Ontario, Canada	Oxford OX3 7AD
N.Y. 10118	L0S 1J0	United Kingdom

Cataloguing in Publication Data
Taylor, Dave, 1948-
 Endangered ocean animals

(The endangered animals series)
Includes index.
ISBN 0-86505-533-5 (library bound) ISBN 0-86505-543-2 (pbk.)
Problems such as ocean pollution, oil spills, and hunting have caused marine mammals, birds, and fish to become endangered.

1. Marine fauna - Juvenile literature. 2. Endangered species - Juvenile literature. 3. Wildlife conservation - Juvenile literature. I. Title. II. Series: Taylor, Dave, 1948- . The endangered animals series.

QL122.2.T39 1993   j591.921

Contents

The world's oceans

Three-quarters of the earth is covered by oceans. The three large bodies of water that we call oceans are the Atlantic, Pacific, and Indian oceans. Oceans are important to all living things. They provide food and moisture for the earth and are instrumental in creating our weather. Ocean water evaporates, joins the water cycle, and becomes rain, fog, and snow.

Atmosphere helpers

Another important gift oceans give the earth is **algae**. Algae are tiny one-celled plants that play an essential role in slowing down **global warming**. Scientists believe that the earth is slowly growing warmer because gases, such as **carbon dioxide**, act like a blanket around the earth, preventing heat from escaping.

Absorbing carbon dioxide

Carbon dioxide is produced by car exhaust, industrial pollution, and forest fires. The removal of carbon dioxide from the air helps slow down the warming of the atmosphere. Trees change much carbon dioxide into oxygen, but ocean algae absorb more carbon dioxide than all the earth's rainforests combined!

Ocean pollution

Each year trillions of tons of sewage and dangerous industrial wastes are dumped into the oceans. Beaches are polluted by plastic litter and medical waste. Oil spills damage fragile ocean ecosystems. These harmful wastes kill thousands of species of fish, plants, and other marine creatures.

A threat to all life

Ocean pollution threatens everyone. Although many of us do not live near an ocean, the fish we eat, the air we breathe, and the temperature of our earth are all affected by ocean pollution. Isn't it time to protect the oceans of the world and the animals that live in it?

Animals in danger

In recent years people have forced many kinds of animals to struggle for survival. Hunting, farming, and the loss of wilderness areas have made life difficult and sometimes impossible for thousands of species of animals.

Terms of endangerment

Worldwide conservation groups use various terms to describe animals in distress. Animals that are **extinct** have not been seen in the wild for over 50 years. Animals referred to as **endangered** are likely to die out if their situation is not improved. **Threatened** animals are endangered in some areas where they live. Animals that are **vulnerable** may soon move into the endangered category if the causes that put them in danger are not corrected. **Rare** animals are species with small populations that may be at risk.

Endangered ocean animals

There is reason to be concerned about all ocean animals. Even if some species are not yet threatened or endangered, they may lose their lives because of pollution or commercial fishing.

There is hope, however. Due to the efforts of conservation groups, many animals that once faced extinction are surviving in healthy populations again.

Walruses can be found throughout the ice floes of the Canadian Arctic, Alaska, and northern Russia. They are endangered because of overhunting. These large relatives of the seal family were killed for their ivory tusks and for their blubber, which was made into oil.

The humpback whale

Whales are the largest animals on earth. They look like fish, but they are actually warm-blooded mammals. Whales nurse their babies and breathe air, as we do. Some whales even sing!

Many whales are now endangered. The humpback is one of these whales. There are fewer than 10,000 humpbacks left in the oceans of the world. Whaling has put them in danger of extinction.

Teeth or no teeth?

There are two families of whales: toothed and toothless. The humpback whale belongs to the toothless, or **baleen** family. Baleen are long, rough, hairy growths that hang down from the roof of the whale's mouth and help collect food. As the whale swims, the baleen act as a sieve, trapping huge amounts of krill, plankton, and tiny fish. Baleen whales grow much larger than toothed whales.

Underwater operas

Humpback whales are famous for their eerie songs. These songs can last as long as 30 minutes! Scientists have discovered that solitary males sing these songs in their winter breeding grounds, although they are not sure why. One theory is that these whales are singing to attract mates.

The sad story of whaling

The hunting of the humpback whale has been going on since prehistoric times. During the nineteenth century, the demand for whale products grew and so did the whaling industry.

Over two million whales were killed in commercial whale hunts! **Blubber**, which is the fatty material beneath the whale's skin, was boiled down into oil for lamps. Baleen was used to make many items, ranging from wagon springs to women's undergarments.

The killing continues

In 1966 laws were passed against the whaling of humpbacks. Under this protection, their population has slowly increased, but the killing of whales continues. Some countries have tried to get around the laws by saying they are involved only in "scientific whaling." They argue that they are catching whales to study them but, in fact, the whales are cut up and sold for profit. If humpback whales continue to be hunted, they may become extinct. It would be sad if the singing of these whales were lost to future generations!

Length: 57 feet (17.5 meters)
Weight: 10.5 tons (10,670 kilograms)
Where it lives: The Atlantic and north Pacific oceans

a humpback whale

(above) Humpback whales can hold their breath underwater for up to one hour. They breathe through **blowholes,** *which are like nostrils at the top of their head. Their warm breath blows a cloud of vapor that can be seen from far away. (below) Scientists use photographs of the humpback's tail to identify individual animals. Each whale's tale is as unique as your fingerprints.*

The Steller sea lion

The Steller sea lion is the largest of the **eared seals**, a family that includes sea lions and fur seals. Other seals are called **true seals**. There are two ways to tell these two families apart. 1. As their name suggests, eared seals have small ears, whereas true seals have ear openings. 2. Eared seals can walk on their four limbs and can even run if necessary. True seals cannot walk on land. Instead, they must "hump" their bodies across rocks and beaches.

Few sea lions left

The story of the Steller sea lion is a familiar one. Once, this marine mammal was found throughout the northern coasts of the Pacific Ocean, but in some areas its population is declining rapidly.

Hunted for their oil

In the early 1800s many Steller sea lions lived along the California coast. When settlers moved to California, they discovered that sea lion blubber could provide them with a ready source of oil. Before electrical lights were invented, great quantities of oil were needed for lamps. Between three and four sea lions were killed to make one barrel of oil. By the 1870s the sea lion population on the California coast was drastically reduced.

Shoot on sight!

Steller sea lions faced other problems as well. In 1899 the California Fisheries Commission announced that these seals were interfering with the state's fishing industry and should be shot on sight. One year later, another study revealed that sea lions had very little negative effect on the fishing industry. Unfortunately, this study did not change attitudes about Steller sea lions. People still believed that they were harmful. The killing of these sea lions continued into the 1930s, when a law was finally passed to protect them.

A continued decline

California's Steller sea lion population has dropped to fewer than 1000. Since these eared seals are now fully protected, the reason for their continued decline is not clear. Some scientists think that global warming may be responsible. As the temperature of the earth increases, the water in the southern parts of the sea lion's range may be growing too warm for this mammal and the fish it eats.

In Alaskan waters, the population of Steller sea lions has decreased by 82 percent. Between 1963 and 1972, 45,000 pups were killed for their coats. In 1990 all Steller sea lion populations were listed as threatened, but this has not helped these mammals. Fishing crews still kill sea lions when they come too close to a net.

Length: 11-12 feet (3.3-3.5 meters)
Weight: 600-2300 pounds (272-1043 kilograms)
Where it lives: The northern Pacific coasts

(opposite) In the late spring and summer male sea lions come ashore on isolated parts of the coast and claim a territory. When other males arrive, the first males must fight to keep the best spots and the right to breed with the females. Even after the young sea lions are born, the **rookeries,** *or breeding grounds, remain violent places. Angry males often toss newborn pups if they get in the way, and some pups are crushed as the males chase each other. (right) This sea lion looks more interested in sleeping than fighting!*

The brown pelican

There are seven species of pelicans in the world. All, except the brown pelican, like to live in freshwater lakes. This bird prefers the ocean, where it can feed off the fish that live there. The brown pelican is familiar to anyone who has vacationed on the beaches of the southern United States. The sight of this prehistoric-looking bird soaring over the ocean and diving from great heights is unforgettable.

A stunning dive!

Just before the pelican hits the water, its wings fold back and its neck shoots forward. Special air sacks on the pelican's chest cushion the bird as it comes into contact with the surface of the ocean. The blow of the diving bird stuns the fish. The pelican then uses its huge mouth like a net to scoop them up. The water drains out of its beak, and the fish remain.

Deadly DDT

Brown pelicans are an endangered species because of a chemical called DDT. This chemical was used to control insects in the 1950s. When DDT entered the ecosystem, it had a devastating effect on wildlife. Birds that ate insects built up harmful amounts of this chemical in their bodies and either died or could not reproduce.

Although brown pelicans do not eat insects, they were still affected by DDT. When waste from DDT factories was dumped into the oceans, small fish were poisoned by the chemical. As the pelicans ate the fish, they also ate the dangerous DDT. The eggs laid by female pelicans were weakened by this harmful chemical. The eggshells cracked upon being laid, and the baby pelicans inside died.

Greatly reduced populations

Before DDT was dumped into the oceans, 5000 pairs of brown pelicans were counted on one California island alone. That number was reduced to 100 in 1968 and then to 12 in 1969. By the 1970s the brown pelican had almost vanished from California, Texas, and Louisiana. In Florida the brown pelican had a different problem. In that state, developers destroyed pelican nesting sites to build houses, resorts, and condominiums.

Will this bird survive?

In 1972 the use of DDT was restricted by law. Even though the effects of the chemical have left the ecosystem, the brown pelican population has not yet recovered. Scientists believe that many of the fish that the brown pelican eats have been killed by the warming climate, which is a result of pollution. The future of this bird does not look promising!

Length: 48 inches (122 centimeters)
Wingspan: 84 inches (213 centimeters)
Where it lives: The tropical and subtropical coasts of the United States, Mexico, Central America, and South America

---

During their first year pelicans are brown. They turn greyish in their second year. By the time they are three, they take on adult colors.

Pelicans build their nests close together in trees or mangroves. In these nests the chicks hatch without feathers. They look like baby dinosaurs! The first chicks to hatch are the largest. They steal food from their younger brothers and sisters. Unless there is enough food for all the chicks, the largest are the only ones likely to survive to adulthood.

The harbor seal

Harbor seals live along northern coasts around the world. Unfortunately, these animals are decreasing in number. In some areas, they are already extinct. The decline in the harbor seal's number is due to oil spills, pollution of coastal areas, and the killing of seals by fishing crews who believe that the seals compete for fish.

True seals

Harbor seals belong to the family of true seals. Like all seals and sea lions, harbor seals find their food in the sea, but they must come to land to breed and give birth. They cannot walk on land as sea lions can. To move on land, they must "hump" themselves forward.

New pups

Once a year harbor seals shed their hair. This is called **molting**. Their breeding season begins soon after they molt. Males mate when they are six years old and females when they are three or four. Harbor seal pups are born on shore away from other seals. They usually weigh about 24 pounds (11 kilograms) and can swim almost immediately.

Covered with blubber

Harbor seals are covered by thick blubber and a thin layer of hair. The blubber allows these animals to live in very cold water. Although they possess this excellent insulator, harbor seals prefer to stay away from the ice floes of the north. They live farther south than any other seal except the monk seal.

> **Length**: 4-5.5 feet (1.2-1.7 meters)
> **Weight**: 550 pounds (250 kilograms)
> **Where it lives**: The north Atlantic and Pacific coasts

In the water, harbor seals are quite agile. Their powerful hind flippers propel them with ease. On land, however, these seals cannot move as easily as their eared seal relatives can.

The California sea lion

The California sea lion lives in two separate areas of the world. One population is on the coast of California south to Baja, Mexico. It now numbers over 40,000 animals. The second population is in the Galapagos Islands off the coast of Ecuador. About 20,000 California sea lions live there.

California sea lions breed in June and July. After the breeding season is over, the males travel together and do not see the females or the pups for another year. When at sea, these sea lions leap like dolphins out of the water. When they rest, they float on the surface of the ocean in groups called **rafts**.

Where is my mom?

After giving birth on land, the female sea lions go back to sea to feed. If they cannot find their own pups when they return, the pups will die. No female will feed any pup other than its own. If one is bothered by a lost pup, she will grab it by the scruff of its neck and toss it away.

Brush with extinction

The story of the California sea lion's brush with extinction is similar in many ways to that of the Steller sea lion's. California sea lions were also targets of the seal hunters.

Although this sea lion is smaller than the Steller sea lion, it existed in greater numbers. California sea lions were easy to hunt because their rookeries were on California's mainland beaches.

Increasing in number

Today, the California sea lion population is much lower than it was 200 years ago, but it is increasing because of protection laws. The recovery of this sea lion shows that endangered animals can grow in number again!

> **Length**: Female: up to 6 feet (1.8 meters) Male: 6.5-8 feet (2-2.5 meters)
> **Weight**: Female: under 220 pounds (100 kilograms) Male: 600 pounds (272 kilograms)
> **Where it lives**: The Pacific coast of North America and the Galapagos Islands

Male California sea lions bark constantly and can be heard from several miles away. They bark about three times a second. Females bark less than the males, but their bark has a wider vocal range.

Sharks

Shark! The very word strikes terror in the hearts of many people. Sharks have been the subject of books and movies, but the truth is not as scary. There are around 350 kinds of sharks, and only 30 types are known to attack people. There are fewer than 100 attacks reported each year, and less than 30 are fatal. Sharks don't actually eat people. They take a bite and spit it out. Scientists believe that sharks don't like the taste of human flesh. Of course, even a small bite from a shark can be deadly!

Looking for food

Sharks prefer to find their food among other ocean animals. Most sharks eat fish, although larger sharks prey on sea mammals. Some sharks bury themselves in the sand and lie there waiting for food to come along. Others prowl the open ocean hunting for a meal.

The smell of blood!

Sharks have nerve endings along their entire body. These nerve endings are called the **lateral line**. Sharks can feel unusual vibrations in the water with these nerves and can tell if the animal or fish making the vibrations is injured. Sharks also use their fine-tuned sense of smell and follow their noses to find prey. A shark can smell a single drop of blood in an area of ocean as large as a classroom. They also have good eyes. When sharks get close to their prey, they can see it even in the dark.

Jaws!

No one ever thought sharks would become endangered and need protection, but in the 1970s a book and movie popularized the hunting of sharks to the point that their population has dropped drastically. Why? Many people believe that sharks are dangerous. Statistics show, however, that millions more sharks are eaten by people than the other way around. Sharks should be the ones that are terrified!

Shark survival

Sharks swam the oceans over 350 million years ago, long before dinosaurs ever roamed the earth. They could survive for a long time to come, if human beings left them alone. As long as people continue to kill sharks for food and sport, sharks will continue to decrease in number. Some scientists fear that it may already be too late to save them.

Length: 6 inches-60 feet (15 centimeters-18 meters)
Where they live: In all the oceans of the world

(opposite top) The hammerhead shark's head resembles a hammer. Its nostrils and eyes are spread apart at either end of the head to allow this shark to track scents more efficiently. (bottom left) Most sharks have between four and six rows of teeth. Some have up to twenty rows. Sharks constantly lose their teeth when they feed. New teeth grow in to replace lost ones. A single shark may have over 10,000 teeth during its lifetime. (bottom right) The leopard shark is considered harmless to humans.

Dolphins

There are more than 50 species of dolphins. The smallest is the Heaviside's dolphin, and the largest is the orca, or killer whale. All dolphins have teeth and belong to the family of **toothed whales**.

Dolphins live in all the world's oceans, and a few types can even be found in freshwater rivers such as the Amazon River in South America and the Indus River in Pakistan.

Echolocation
Dolphins navigate through the ocean by using **echolocation**. They produce a series of clicks that travel as soundwaves through the water. The soundwaves hit an object and reflect back, just as your voice echoes off a cave wall. The returning "echo" tells the dolphin the location, size, and shape of a fish. Dolphins also use echolocation to avoid enemies such as sharks.

Dangerous nets
The main reason dolphins are endangered is because of a fishing method developed in the 1950s. Fishing crews would spot dolphins feeding above a school of tuna fish, circle the school,

drop their nets, and capture both the tuna and the dolphins. Sadly, the dolphins they hauled in were either drowned or crushed in the machinery before they could be released.

By 1972 nearly four million dolphins had been killed by this fishing method, and many injured dolphins escaped only to die later. In the 1970s laws were passed to stop this terrible practice, but they were not enforced. Dolphins continued to be killed in large numbers.

No tuna for lunch!

The future of the dolphin looked uncertain until a terrible event caught the attention of the world. In 1987 a tuna boat killed between 200 and 300 Costa Rican spinner dolphins, which made up half the population of this rare species! These terrible killings were filmed, and the film was shown on television.

It was discovered that during the 1980s 113,000 dolphins were killed in nets each year. Many people were so outraged that they stopped buying tuna. This forced tuna companies to use other methods of tuna fishing that don't hurt dolphins. Unfortunately, some fishing crews still use the old harmful methods.

Difficult to protect

Every dolphin population has declined in recent years. Even though a country can protect the dolphins living near its coast, little can be done to help the ones that are outside coastal waters. Protecting dolphins in these waters requires an agreement among several countries, which is very difficult to negotiate.

Other problems

Dolphins face other problems as well. Ocean pollution and decreasing numbers of fish are reducing their populations. Much is being done to save dolphins, but only time will tell if these efforts succeed.

Length: 3.5-31 feet (1-9 meters)
Weight: 88-9920 pounds (40-4500 kilograms)
Where they live: Warm water ocean areas

Many people confuse the terms dolphin and porpoise. Although these two mammals are related, they look quite different. A porpoise (right) is smaller than a dolphin (opposite) and has a rounded snout. It has no beak, and its teeth are spade-shaped. A dolphin has more pointed teeth in both jaws. It has a rounded forehead, called a **melon**, *and possesses a beaklike snout.*

The southern sea otter

Sea otters are mammals that belong to the weasel family. They are the only members of this family that rely on the sea for all their food.

Shallow water

A sea otter's habitat is restricted by the depth of the ocean. Although sea otters can dive to a depth of 180 feet (55 meters), they prefer water that is not much deeper than 115 feet (35 meters). Female sea otters stay in shallower areas, whereas the males often head out to deeper seas.

Bloody noses

Female sea otters are easy to recognize because they have scarred or bloody noses. During mating season, the male sea otter bites the nose of the female and holds on tight. Males do this for two reasons. Biting prevents the female from escaping and keeps her near the surface of the water so both animals can breathe.

Sociable males

Male sea otters are more sociable than the females. Rafts of over 1000 males have been reported, and sightings of over 100 are common. A large female raft contains only about 20 females and their young.

Where have all the otters gone?

Once sea otters could be found on most north Pacific coasts. Today they are gone from most of that range, existing only in small isolated groups. The sea otter

population has declined because this animal was hunted for its beautiful fur. In the nineteenth century, Russian explorers began trading for sea otter pelts with the native people that lived along the coast. The thick fur of the otter is so fine that it quickly became popular among fashionable people.

American and English fur traders also began hunting and trapping the otters. It wasn't long before these animals became rare. Unfortunately, this only made otter fur even more valuable! It looked as if the species would soon become extinct!

Almost extinct

In 1911 international laws were passed to protect the sea otter. By this time, over half a million otters had been hunted and nearly three times that many were killed at sea and sank before trappers could recover the pelts. Sea otters were completely wiped out along the western coasts of Canada and California. A few survived in Alaska, but some hunting continued there.

A healthy comeback

In 1938 a group of fifty sea otters was found along the coast of California. Today this group numbers over 1500 animals. The more northerly sea otters number between 150,000 and 200,000. The sea otter has made a healthy comeback, although its future is still uncertain.

The danger of oil spills

Another great danger threatens sea otters—oil spills. When a sea otter gets oil on its fur, it cannot survive very long. The oil ruins the otter's coat, leaving the animal with no protection against the cold. The otter tries to lick the oil off and dies from this poison.

Length: Female: 49 inches (125 centimeters) Male: 53 inches (135 centimeters) **Weight**: Female: 40-55 pounds (18-25 kilograms) Male: 33-100 pounds (15-45 kilograms) **Where it lives**: Along the northern coasts of the Pacific Ocean

Sea otters spend most of their lives in the water. Sometimes they come out on dry land, but such visits are short. These jaunts are called **hauling out***. Sea otters haul out only when they are sick or when the weather is very cold. Male sea otters do not migrate, but they often leave their areas of birth to search for females.*

Preserving ocean life

There are many ways you can help clean up our oceans and protect the animals that live there.

When you go to the beach, even if it is not at the ocean, make sure you do not litter. The garbage will eventually reach the sea, where it affects ocean ecosystems. You might even wish to bring a garbage bag to the beach and clean up the litter that careless people have left behind. You will be doing your part to preserve our oceans.

Be responsible

Make sure that when you or your parents use cleaners or other chemicals outside, that none is spilled on the ground. Every liquid that is dumped eventually ends up in the water. When your parents throw out chemicals such as motor-oil or paint, make sure these dangerous substances are disposed of properly.

Banning balloons

Most schools no longer release helium-filled balloons into the air during special occasions. These balloons ended up in the ocean, killing sharks and dolphins. If you see someone releasing balloons, inform them of the damage balloons can do!

Watching whales has become a popular pastime for tourists on the west coast of North America. Whale watchers go to special locations where these majestic animals swim. They can see whales splash their tail against the water's surface and blow vapor out of their blowhole. It is a thrilling experience to see these endangered animals in the wild!

Writing letters

One of the best ways to help ocean life is to write letters to the government. Encourage your government officials to stop the pollution of oceans. If people show that they care about preserving the ocean ecosystem, the government will also help protect it.

Thinking green

When you go to the grocery store with your parents, encourage them to buy green products. These products often cost more than regular products, but they help decrease waste and pollution. Buying these products shows that you support a healthy planet!

Glossary

algae Tiny plants that live in the ocean

baleen Long growths in the mouths of some whales that are used for collecting food

blowhole A breathing hole located on the top of the heads of whales and dolphins

blubber The layer of fat on some marine mammals such whales and seals

carbon dioxide A gas that is composed of oxygen and carbon and contributes to global warming

commercial Relating to a business or trade

conservation Protection from loss, harm, or waste, especially of natural resources such as wildlife

DDT A dangerous chemical used for controlling insects

echolocation The method used by dolphins and other toothed whales to locate objects in the water

ecosystem A community of living things that are connected to one another and to the surroundings in which they live

endanger To threaten with extinction

environment The setting and conditions in which a living being exists

extinct Not in existence; not seen in the wild for over 50 years

Galapagos Islands An island group located off the coast of Ecuador

global warming The theory that the earth is getting warmer because of pollution

groom To make neat and tidy in appearance

habitat The natural environment of a plant or animal

krill Small ocean animals with shells

mammal A warm-blooded animal that has a backbone and hair on its body

mangrove Tropical evergreen trees found in marshy areas

melon The rounded forehead of the dolphin

molt To shed feathers, skin, or hair in preparation for new growth

nurse To feed a baby with mother's milk

plankton Tiny plants and animals that drift in the sea

pollution Something that makes the environment impure or dirty

population The people or animals of an area; the total number of individuals living in a particular area

prey An animal that is hunted by another animal for food

raft A group of animals floating on the surface of the ocean

rainforest A dense forest in an area of heavy annual rainfall

range An area over which an animal roams and finds food

rare Uncommon; in serious danger of becoming extinct

reduce To make smaller

rookery A colony or breeding ground for seals or birds

sewage Human waste

species A group of related plants or animals that can produce young together

threatened Describing an animal that is endangered in some parts of its habitat

tropical Hot and humid; describing an area close to the equator

vulnerable Capable of becoming endangered

wean To make a young animal accustomed to eating food other than its mother's milk

Index

2 3 4 5 6 7 8 9 0   Printed in USA   2 1 0 9 8 7 6 5 4 3